CHRIS PACKHAM

AMAZING ANIMAL
BABIES

ILLUSTRATED BY JASON COCKCROFT

STERLING CHILDREN'S BOOKS
New York

Every day, hundreds of thousands of human babies
are born around the world, just as you were.

duck

duckling

And at the same time, billions of other creatures
are also starting their lives, but not all in quite
the same way that you did.

Most mammals, such as orangutans and humans, grow inside their mother and suckle milk when they are born.

orangutan

Other animals hatch from hard- or soft-shelled eggs.

golden eagle chick

Unlike humans, many fish and insects produce huge numbers of eggs all at once.

sockeye salmon

seahorse

And for a few types of animals, such as the seahorse, it is the male, rather than the female, that gives birth to young.

fry

Some baby animals are looked after
by their parents or family group
for many years as they grow up.

elephant

calf

Others have to fend
for themselves as soon
as they are born.

stick insect

Would you like to meet some more amazing baby animals?

DARWIN'S FROGS live in forest streams in Chile and Argentina. After the female has laid her eggs, the male guards them, gulping them up when they start moving and keeping them safely in his mouth.

froglet

The eggs hatch into tiny tadpoles after a few days. Once they have grown into hopping froglets, the adult male spits them out into the big wide world.

Not all parents take such good care of their offspring. On an island in Indonesia lurks the largest lizard in the world — the **KOMODO DRAGON**.

The Komodo dragon is so big that it can eat deer and even humans. The adults may also eat their own babies!

To avoid being gobbled up by their parents, young Komodo dragons climb nearby trees because the adults are too heavy to climb after them. They don't risk coming down until they are at least two years old!

To help stop their parents eating them, the babies also roll in smelly dung.

BLACK-FOOTED ALBATROSS chicks from
Hawaii also have to be extremely brave at an early age.
At just five months old these seabirds head for the ocean.
They will spend most of their lives swooping above the water.

Young birds that have
just learned to fly are
called fledglings.

tiger shark

The chicks aren't able to fly very well at first and have to watch out for cunning tiger sharks that know the tired fledglings will land on the waves to rest.

Around one in ten albatross chicks ends up in the growling tummy of a shark.

TIGER cubs need up to two years with their mothers to learn how to hunt and survive.

chital deer

If cubs are orphaned from six months they may still have a chance of reaching adulthood, but they have to rely on these natural qualities:

Their night vision enables them to hunt in low light.

Their claws and teeth are perfect weapons for grasping and killing prey.

Their stripes help them to hide in the grasslands and forests.

One creature that needs its coat for more than just hiding is the **POLAR BEAR**. Temperatures in the Arctic can drop below -76°F — brrrrrr!

Cubs are born in underground snow
dens and grow long fur with a thick
woolly undercoat to keep them cozy.
Their paws even have furry undersides!

Cubs stay with their mother
for about two and a half years.

COBRAS live in Africa, Australia, and Southern Asia. These cold-blooded animals need heat from their surroundings to keep warm. Cobras lay their eggs in a nest to help keep them toasty.

egg tooth

1. Eggs are laid somewhere safe and warm.

2. An "egg tooth" on its snout helps the baby hatch.

3. A newborn cobra has to look after itself.

4. Baby cobras can defend themselves with a poisonous bite just like the adults.

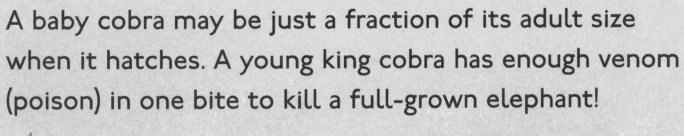

A baby cobra may be just a fraction of its adult size when it hatches. A young king cobra has enough venom (poison) in one bite to kill a full-grown elephant!

The venom comes from fangs in the cobra's mouth.

When threatened, the cobra shows its "hood."

mongoose

Most cobras eat small creatures, such as rats, birds, and lizards.

RATS can be very common and are eaten by many animals, so they spend lots of time under the ground. But they come out at night to look for food.

Although baby rats don't open their eyes until they leave the nest at two weeks old, scientists have discovered that their sense of direction is already almost as good as their parents'.

Unlike rats, we aren't able to recognize and remember our world until we are about six months old.

The sun-scorched deserts of Southern Africa are home to **MEERKATS**. They also live underground, where it is cooler. The pups love eating scorpions, but their stings can be deadly, so adults bring pups dead scorpions to practice with before they make their first kill.

The pups also eat juicy worms and other small creatures.

When the pups move on to live scorpions, they must strike quickly and bite off the stinger just to be safe. They also have to dodge the scorpion's powerful pincers!

stinger

pincers

worm eggs

There are over 3,000 species of **EARTHWORM**. The longest, measuring over 22 feet, is found in South Africa. However, you can see smaller ones in your backyard. Some worms are ready to lay their own eggs just ten weeks after they emerge from their silky cocoons as babies.

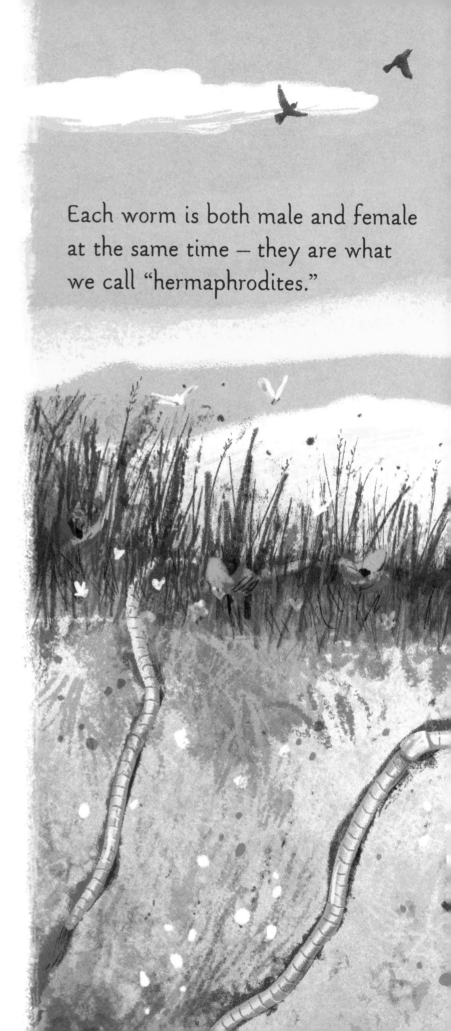

Each worm is both male and female at the same time — they are what we call "hermaphrodites."

As you have seen, the world is full of amazing baby animals and many are growing up in your neighborhood, so you can be a part of their magical lives. Just like you, each animal is a unique individual with a story to tell.

Baby earthworms hatch from cocoons that are smaller than a grain of rice.

DISCOVER MORE

BLACK-FOOTED ALBATROSSES

Black-footed albatrosses are often attracted to the fins of sharks, as well as floating plastic and other waste objects in the sea. Interestingly though, they are known to avoid ships in areas where they have been cruelly treated by humans.

COBRAS

Cobra is a word for "snake." When threatened, these snakes show their "hood," which is an extension of their neck ribs. This is to try and scare off predators as it makes them look bigger. Snakes lay their soft eggs in a safe, warm place and then leave them to hatch.

DARWIN'S FROGS

Darwin's frogs lay up to 40 eggs at a time. These frogs were discovered in the forests of South America in the 1830s by the famous English naturalist Charles Darwin. Like many amphibians, they are now at risk due to a very dangerous killer fungus.

EARTHWORMS

The best way to tell if a worm is a baby or adult, apart from size, is to see if it has a thick band around it (called a clitellum) as only the adults have this. Unlike humans, earthworms don't have a hard skeleton so they contract their muscles in waves to propel themselves forwards.

ELEPHANTS

Elephants live in family groups of 10–20 individuals. Females are pregnant for 22 months, and their calves suckle their milk for up to five years. The babies' trunks are floppy until their muscles have developed, then they use them to suck up water and shovel food into their mouths.

GOLDEN EAGLES

The golden eagle, a fierce bird of prey, practices "siblicide"—where the oldest chick kills its younger brothers or sisters. This behavior is common when there's not much food as it means the survivor will have less competition for every meal.

KOMODO DRAGONS

Like cobra babies, komodo dragon babies are born with a special "egg tooth." This acts like a power tool helping them to cut themselves free of the leathery egg that protects them while they develop. It falls off soon after they hatch.

MEERKATS

Adult meerkats have developed immunity to the deadly venom of some scorpions, but pups still need to be careful of a scorpion's sting.

ORANGUTANS

Orangutans spend most of their day swinging through branches high above the rainforest floor. Babies must cling to their mothers' bellies for four months.

POLAR BEARS

Polar bears are the largest land carnivores. Cubs feast on creamy milk that has loads of fat to help them grow quickly and keep them warm in the Arctic. Seals are their favorite food, and they can smell them on floating pack ice up to 3,200 feet away.

RATS

Rats are found everywhere in the world, except for Antarctica. A rat's sense of direction is important as these rodents live in complex underground mazes, such as sewer systems. Many people keep rats as pets, and we now know that pups make giggling noises when they play or are tickled!

SEAHORSES

Seahorses may not look like fish, but they are. When males and females mate they dance with each other and change color before the female lays her eggs inside the male's tummy. He later gives birth to miniature seahorses.

STERLING CHILDREN'S BOOKS
New York

An Imprint of Sterling Publishing Co., Inc.
1166 Avenue of the Americas
New York, NY 10036

STERLING CHILDREN'S BOOKS and the distinctive Sterling Children's Books logo are
trademarks of Sterling Publishing Co., Inc.

Text © 2017 by Chris Packham
Illustrations © 2017 Jason Cockcroft

All rights reserved. No part of this publication may be reproduced, stored in a retrieval system,
or transmitted in any form or by any means (including electronic, mechanical, photocopying,
recording, or otherwise) without prior written permission from the publisher.

ISBN 978-1-4549-2337-4

Distributed in Canada by Sterling Publishing
c/o Canadian Manda Group, 664 Annette Street
Toronto, Ontario, Canada M6S 2C8

For information about custom editions, special sales, and premium and corporate purchases,
please contact Sterling Special Sales at 800-805-5489 or specialsales@sterlingpublishing.com.

Manufactured in Malaysia
Lot #:
2 4 6 8 10 9 7 5 3 1
11/16

www.sterlingpublishing.com